For Chris

Printed in Italy.

First U.S. Edition 1986
1 2 3 4 5 6 7 8 9 10

Library of Congress Cataloging in Publication Data
Ormerod, Jan.
   The story of Chicken Licken.
   Summary: "Chicken Licken" is retold with
illustrations of school children performing the
story as a play on stage.
   [1. Folklore]   I. Title.
PZ8.1.062St   1986   398.2'4528617 [F]   85-7911
ISBN 0-688-06058-7

THE STORY OF
CHICKEN LICKEN

by
**Jan
Ormerod**

Lothrop, Lee & Shepard Books

New York

OH, HENNY PENNY, DON'T GO!

I was going and the sky fell

on my poor little head.

Now I am going to tell the king.

OH, COCK LOCK, DON'T GO!

I was going and I met Chicken

Licken and the sky had fallen

on her poor little head.

Now we are going to tell the king.

OH, DUCK LUCK, DON'T GO!
I was going and I met Henny Penny,
and Henny Penny met Chicken Licken
and the sky had fallen
on her poor little head.
Now we are going to tell the king.

OH, DRAKE LAKE, DON'T GO!

I was going and I met Cock Lock,

and Cock Lock met Henny Penny,

and Henny Penny met Chicken Licken

and the sky had fallen

on her poor little head.

Now we are going to tell the king.

OH, GOOSE LOOSE, DON'T GO!

I was going and I met Duck Luck,

and Duck Luck met Cock Lock,

and Cock Lock met Henny Penny,

and Henny Penny met Chicken Licken

and the sky had fallen

on her poor little head.

Now we are going to tell the king.

OH, GANDER LANDER, DON'T GO!

I was going and I met Drake Lake,

and Drake Lake met Duck Luck,

and Duck Luck met Cock Lock,

and Cock Lock met Henny Penny,

and Henny Penny met Chicken Licken

and the sky had fallen

on her poor little head.

Now we are going to tell the king.

So Gander Lander turned back
and met Turkey Lurkey.
He asked Turkey Lurkey
where he was going.

I am going
to the woods
for some food.

OH, TURKEY LURKEY, DON'T GO!

I was going and I met Goose Loose,

and Goose Loose met Drake Lake,

and Drake Lake met Duck Luck,

and Duck Luck met Cock Lock,

and Cock Lock met Henny Penny,

and Henny Penny met

Chicken Licken and the sky

had fallen on her poor little head.

Now we are going to tell the king.

So Turkey Lurkey turned back and walked with Gander Lander, Goose Loose, Drake Lake, Duck Luck, Cock Lock, Henny Penny and Chicken Licken. As they were going along they met Foxy Woxy.

Where are you going?

Chicken Licken went to the woods
and the sky fell
on her poor little head.
Now we are going to tell the king.

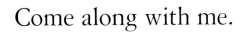

Foxy Woxy took them

into the fox's hole.

He and his young ones

soon ate up poor Chicken Licken,

Henny Penny, Cock Lock, Duck Luck,

Drake Lake, Goose Loose,

Gander Lander and Turkey Lurkey.

So they never saw the king

and they never told him

that the sky had fallen.